T0016713

5-Minute
Jesus Stories

5-Minute
Jesus Stories

Written and Illustrated by
Diego Jourdan Pereira

Good Books

New York, New York

To my Great-great-grandfather,
LUIS JOURDAN.

His light still shines in the darkness.

Copyright © 2023 by Diego Jourdan Pereira

All rights reserved. No part of this book may be reproduced in any manner without the express written consent of the publisher, except in the case of brief excerpts in critical reviews or articles. All inquiries should be addressed to Good Books, 307 West 36th Street, 11th Floor, New York, NY 10018.

Good Books books may be purchased in bulk at special discounts for sales promotion, corporate gifts, fund-raising, or educational purposes. Special editions can also be created to specifications. For details, contact the Special Sales Department, Good Books, 307 West 36th Street, 11th Floor, New York, NY 10018 or info@skyhorsepublishing.com.

Good Books is an imprint of Skyhorse Publishing, Inc.®, a Delaware corporation.

Visit our website at www.goodbooks.com.

10 9 8 7 6 5 4 3

Library of Congress Cataloging-in-Publication Data is available on file.

Print ISBN: 978-1-68099-894-8
EBook ISBN: 978-1-68099-899-3

Interior abridgment and illustrations by Diego Jourdan Pereira
Cover design by Kai Texel

Printed in China

5-Minute
Jesus Stories

Table of Contents

Note to Parents

"And the child grew and became strong, filled with wisdom. And the favor of God was upon him."
—Luke 2:40 (ESV)

The book you're now holding is only a bedtime introduction to the life of Christ Jesus, its pages a means to introduce small children to our Savior's love and sacrifice. In no way should it be taken as a substitute for the faithful reading of the four gospels presented to us by Matthew, Mark, Luke, and John. Hence, corresponding chapters and verses have been referenced at the beginning of each story.

Loving care has been given to harmonize Gospel narratives while keeping contents friendly for younger readers. I am particularly grateful to BiblicalTraining.org for informing my research, while my editor's unwavering support and watchful eye did the rest.

Artistically, my illustration style rests on the shoulders of giants, starting with Eastern Orthodox icon painters and ending with modern-era cartoonist Hergé (Georges Remi, 1907–1983), but the enduring influence of my apprenticeship under master Mariano Ramos cannot be overstated. Mariano made me the artist I am today.

Last but not least, no author should pass on the chance to publicly testify his love and reverence for the Son of Man, and yours truly is no exception. Hence, any flaws you may find within are my own. As for any value drawn from these pages, *soli Deo gloria*.

—Diego Jourdan Pereira

Gabriel Visits Mary and Joseph

Matthew 1:18-24, Luke 1:26-38

Two thousand years ago,
God sent the angel Gabriel
on a mission to Nazareth,
a village nested against the
mountains of Galilee.

A young woman named Mary was startled
when the angel appeared before her.
"Do not be afraid," Gabriel told Mary.
"You will give birth to a son, and you will
name him Jesus. He will be called Son of God and his kingdom will never end."

"I am a servant of the Lord; let this be as you say," replied Mary. At that
very instant she became pregnant by the power of the Holy Spirit.

But Mary was already engaged to a carpenter named Joseph. He was a good
man, but when he found his future wife was with child he did
not know what to do.

So Gabriel appeared to him in a dream and
said, "Joseph, son of David, do not be afraid
to wed Mary. She will have a son, and you
will name him Jesus. And Jesus will save
people from their sins."

When Joseph awoke, he did as the
angel of the Lord asked. He married
Mary and adopted Jesus as his
own boy.

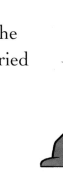

The Birth of Jesus

Matthew 1:25, Luke 2:1-10

Around the time Gabriel visited Mary and Joseph, Roman Emperor Caesar Augustus wanted to find out how many people lived under his rule, so he ordered everyone to be counted.

People had to register at their original family hometown. Since Joseph was the great-great-great-great-great grandson of King David, who was born in a town called Bethlehem, Joseph and Mary had to travel there.

With baby Jesus due any time, after a long journey they finally made it to Bethlehem, but the town was overflowing with people arriving to register also.

Without a place to sleep on this chilly night, Joseph and Mary found refuge inside a cave, which in those days was used as a stable for farm animals.

There, Mary gave birth to a beautiful

baby boy she wrapped in cloths and, having no crib, carefully laid him into a manger filled with hay.

Out in the Bethlehem fields, shepherds kept watch over their flock when an angel of the Lord appeared before them surrounded by blinding light. The men were really scared, but the angel said, "Don't be afraid, I bring you news of great joy for all. A Savior was born tonight, and you will find him laying in a manger."

Then many angels appeared alongside the first one, singing praises to the Lord.

"Glory to God in the highest, and on earth peace among those with whom he is pleased!"

Without delay, the shepherds headed for Bethlehem and found baby Jesus with his parents, like the angel said.

The Three Wise Men

Matthew 2:1-12

Meanwhile, beyond Bethlehem, beyond Galilee, and even beyond the borders of Palestine, wise men from the East saw the Savior's rising star in the night sky. They followed it through deserts and mountains, and when they reached Jerusalem they asked, "Where has the King of the Jews been born?"

Their question put evil King Herod on high alert. Self-important as he was insecure, he dreaded the appearance of the Messiah, fearing he would steal his thunder, so Herod called the wise men to his palace.

"Go to Bethlehem and search everywhere for the child. Then send word to me of his whereabouts, so I may come and worship him myself," he told them.

Finally reaching Bethlehem, the wise men saw the star coming to rest over the new place where baby Jesus was and they rejoiced. When they saw baby Jesus with Mary they fell down to worship him and offered three sets of gifts:

Gold for his kingship.

Frankincense for his divinity.

And myrrh for his future sacrifice.

The wise men secretly returned East following a different route, so Herod wouldn't know where baby Jesus was.

The Holy Family in Egypt

Matthew 2:13-23, Luke 2:39

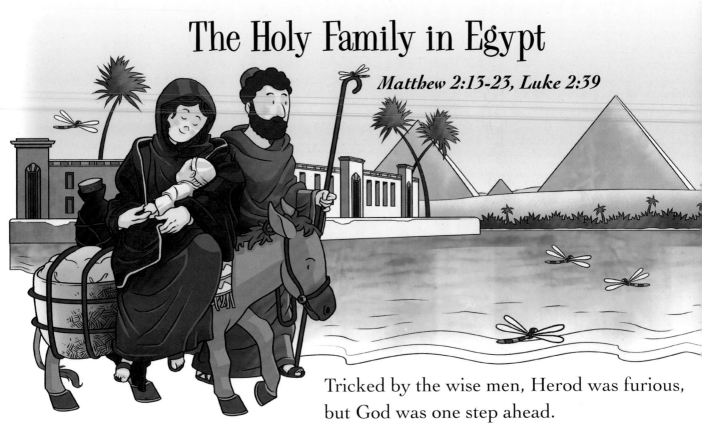

Tricked by the wise men, Herod was furious, but God was one step ahead.

That very night, an angel appeared to Joseph in a dream and warned him of Herod's intentions; so Joseph woke Mary and baby Jesus up and they fled to Egypt, where the mad king wouldn't find them.

It was a long, hard journey south for the young parents and their baby. The desert days were hot, the nights bitter cold, and the road full of robbers, but they made it to the Nile.

The family would stay in Egypt until the angel told Joseph it was now safe to return, because King Herod was dead.

Joseph and Mary considered settling in Judea. However, when they found out the son of King Herod ruled over that region, they decided the safest place to live would be the town of Nazareth, in Galilee, for both of their families still lived there.

Jesus Visits the Temple

Luke 2:41-52

Jesus grew and became strong, helping Joseph at his workshop. Everyone worked hard and did well, and they enjoyed spending the Passover holiday in Jerusalem with the extended family every year.

When Jesus was twelve, he went to Jerusalem with his parents for the festivities, but he stayed behind at the Temple without telling anybody.

After a three-day search, Mary and Joseph finally found the boy sitting among the priests and teachers, joyfully listening to what they had to say and asking questions!

"Son, why did you do this to us?" Mary asked him. "Your father and I have been worried sick searching for you all over town!"

"Why were you looking for me elsewhere?" Jesus replied. "Wasn't it obvious I'd be in my Father's house?"

All the same, he obediently returned with Mary and Joseph to Nazareth, becoming a wise young man.

John Baptizes Jesus

Matthew 3:13-17, Mark 1:9-11, Luke 3:21-23

Jesus had a second cousin named John, the son of Mary's cousin Elizabeth, and a good priest named Zechariah.

When John grew up, he found God in the wild and God gave him a very special mission: he was to prepare the Jewish people for the arrival of Jesus.

So John traveled along the Jordan river, with locusts and wild honey as his only food, and he told people they should treat each other better. Then he baptized them in the waters of the Jordan as a sign of repentance before the coming of the Messiah.

One day, Jesus waded into the Jordan to be baptized by John. The startled prophet said to Jesus, "You should be baptizing me!" But Jesus told him, "Don't say anything, this was God's plan all along."

The Devil Tempts Jesus

Matthew 4:1-11, Mark 1:12-13, Luke 4:1-13

After his baptism, Jesus was led by the Holy Spirit into the desert, where he stayed alone for forty days and forty nights, without any food.

When Jesus felt most hungry, the devil said to him, "If you are the Son of God, command these stones to turn into bread."

But Jesus answered, "Man should not live by bread alone, but by every word that comes from the mouth of God."

When Jesus felt most weak, the devil showed him all the kingdoms of the earth and said, "If you worship me, I will make you king over all of these."

But Jesus answered, "You should worship the Lord your God, and serve only him."

When Jesus felt most lonely, the devil took him to the temple's highest tower and told him, "If you are the Son of God, throw yourself down and his angels will catch you."

But Jesus replied, "Go away, Satan! Don't you test the Lord, your God."

After the devil ran away, wild animals and angels came to keep Jesus company.

Jesus Calls Simon and Andrew

Matthew 4:18-22, Mark 1:16-20, Luke 5:1-11, John 1:35-51

Jesus then returned to Nazareth and began to preach.

"The Kingdom of God has arrived; repent and believe in the good news," he said. But the more popular he became, the more some people were mean to him, so he moved north, to the city of Capernaum, by the Sea of Galilee.

While in Capernaum, Jesus enjoyed walking around the beach. One afternoon, he noticed two fishing boats in the sand, their crews already washing and mending nets after a bad day. He jumped into the boat owned by brothers Andrew and Simon, and asked them to give it one more try.

"We worked night and day and caught nothing, but I will humor you and let down the nets once more" said Simon.

When the brothers did this, the nets caught so much fish they had to call the other boat, manned by brothers James and John, to help them carry the load to shore.

Simon's other name was Peter. Peter, Andrew, James, John, and Jesus soon became close friends.

The Wedding at Cana

John 2:1-11

Jesus and his mother were invited to a wedding in the town of Cana, in Galilee. Mary was already there when Jesus arrived with his new friends from Capernaum, and soon after the wine ran out.

Worried, and a little embarrassed, Mary told Jesus, "They have no wine," expecting him to do something about it. Jesus told her it wasn't time for him to show his power yet, but Mary would have none of it, so she told the catering staff, "Do whatever he tells you."

There were six large stone water jars lying about. "Fill these with water," Jesus said, so the caterers filled them all to the brim. Then Jesus told them, "Now serve some and bring it to your boss for tasting."

When the Head Chef tasted the water, now turned into wine, he rushed to the groom and gave him a sip. "Everyone serves the good wine first," said the startled groom, " but you have kept it until now!"

When the party was over, Mary went with Jesus and his friends to Capernaum for a few days.

Jesus Forgives and Heals a Man

Matthew 9:1-8, Mark 2:1-12, Luke 5:17-26

Back at Capernaum, lots of people were looking for Jesus. When word got around that he was back from Cana, everybody showed up at the place where he was staying. It got so crowded that there was no more room to sit or stand.

Four men also came to the house carrying a friend in a stretcher. He couldn't walk and they wanted Jesus to heal him. When they found they couldn't get through the door, they climbed up on the roof and made an opening through which they lowered down their friend with ropes before Jesus.

Jesus saw they really believed in him, so he said to the man, "Your sins are forgiven."

But the priests and teachers among the crowds didn't believe Jesus was God and were very upset. Seeing the faces they made, Jesus asked them, "Do you think it is easier to say 'your sins are forgiven' than 'get up and walk'?"

So Jesus told the man, "Get up, pick your stretcher, and go home."

The man who couldn't walk did just what Jesus told him, praising God all the way out.

Jesus Calls Levi

Matthew 9:9-13, Mark 2:13-17, Luke 5:27-32

Jesus went out of the house to walk around the shore, and all the people followed him, so they could hear what he had to say.

Passing by the docks, he noticed a man called Levi, also known as Matthew, collecting money inside a Roman tollbooth, and said to him, "Follow me."

Matthew stood up and left everything behind to follow Jesus. He was so happy that he threw a big party at his home, inviting Jesus and all his colleagues from work that evening.

The priests and teachers thought all those who collected money for the Romans were bad people, so they asked Jesus, "Why are you having dinner with Matthew and his friends?"

"Good people don't need any help, but bad people do. Be kind and do not criticize others," replied Jesus.

The Twelve Apostles

Matthew 10:2-4, Mark 3:13-19, Luke 6:12-16

Jesus realized there were so many sick and lost people in Israel, that he couldn't possibly help them all on his own. So he climbed a mountain to find a quiet place to pray.

The next morning, he appointed twelve of his friends as apostles, and sent them out to preach in his name and heal those in need.

"You received without paying, give without pay," he told them, "and make sure you travel light."

The apostles were:

Simon, now called Peter.

Andrew, the brother of Peter.

James, the brother of John.

John, the brother of James.

Philip, a friend of Andrew.

Bartholomew, also called Nathanael.

Thomas, called Didymus.

Levi, called Matthew.

James, the son of Alphaeus.

Jude, called Thaddaeus.

Simon, a known rebel.

And Judas Iscariot, the man who would betray Jesus.

The Beatitudes

Matthew 5:1-12, Luke 6:17-23

When Jesus and the twelve apostles came down from the mountain and stood on the hillside overlooking the fields, they realized a huge crowd of people were already waiting there to hear Jesus's teachings.

So Jesus sat down and said to all:

"Blessed are the poor in spirit, for theirs is the kingdom of heaven.

Blessed are those who mourn, for they will be comforted.

Blessed are the meek, for they will inherit the earth.

Blessed are those who hunger and thirst for justice, for they will be satisfied.

Blessed are the merciful, for they will receive mercy.

Blessed are the pure in heart, for they will see God.

Blessed are the peacemakers, for they will be called sons of God.

Blessed are those who are made to suffer, for the kingdom of heaven belongs to them."

And looking at the twelve, Jesus had one more blessing just for them:

"Blessed are you when others say evil lies about you, and mistreat you for my sake. Be happy and be glad, for there is a great reward waiting for you in heaven."

The Sower

Matthew 13:1-23, Mark 4:1-20, Luke 8:4-15

One day, Jesus went to the beach like he used to, but a large crowd was already there, sitting on the sand as they waited for him. So Jesus got into a boat, and sat in it on the sea to preach comfortably from a distance.

"Listen," he said, "a farmer went out
to sow. As he sowed, some seeds fell
along the path, and the birds came
and ate them."

"Other seeds fell on rocky ground, where they found
little soil. They immediately sprang up, but when the
sun rose, they dried up and withered away."

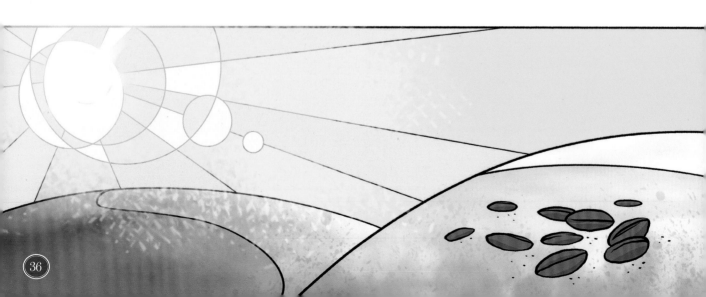

"Other seeds fell among thorns, and the thorns choked them."

"Yet other seeds fell into good ground and grew up, producing a hundred times more grain."

"Do you understand what I'm trying to teach you?" Jesus asked. Most people did not get it, so that evening he explained everything to the apostles.

"I use 'parables' to teach. Parables are stories that help people think about my words and come up with their own answers instead of just telling them," he said.

"In this parable, I am the farmer and I sow God's word. The seeds that fell along the path are the people who hear the word but then the devil comes and snatches it from their hearts. The seeds that fell on rocky ground are those who believe the word of God for a little while, but forget it when life gets hard for them. The seeds that fell among the thorns are those who don't even listen to the word because all they care about is having fun. The seeds that fell into good ground are those who hold tight to the word and never let it go, learning from it with patience over time."

The Mustard Seed

Matthew 13:31-32, Mark 4:30-32, Luke 13:18-19

Jesus and the apostles were walking around town, and he continued to teach them how parables work.

Stopping at a home's front yard he pointed at a large shrub and said, "What can we compare God's plan with?" he asked. "It is like a mustard seed sown into a man's vegetable garden. It is the smallest of seeds, yet when sown it grows into a huge shrub.

And looking under the shrub, he added, "So big, in fact, that the birds from the sky make nests under it."

"What else can we compare God's love for us with?" he said, while they walked a little further.

Stopping by a windowsill, where a loaf of bread was cooling down, he said, "It is like the leaven that a woman mixed with the flour to make this delicious bread puff up."

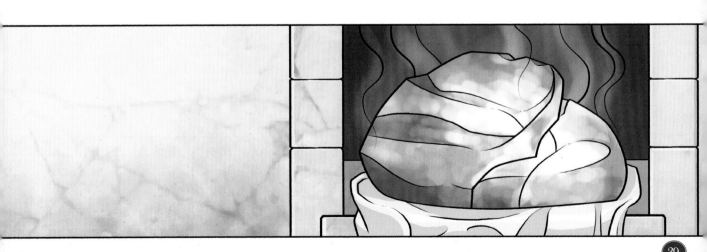

The Treasure and the Pearl

Matthew 13:44-46

Jesus and the apostles continued strolling around town and chanced upon a fenced plot of land.

"God is like a treasure buried in a field which a man finds by accident and buries again. So this man runs back home, gathers all his stuff, sells it, and then uses all the money he made to buy that whole field," Jesus told them.

When Jesus and his friends reached the town market, they stopped by the stalls, filled with the fruits of the sea.

Among them, the pearl merchants drew the biggest crowd, so Jesus added, "Again, finding God is like when a collector of fine pearls sees the one pearl of greatest value in the market and he rushes home, picks all the precious pearls he has in his collection, and then trades them all for the one which is like no other."

Jesus Calms the Storm

Matthew 8:18, 23-27, Mark 4:35-41, Luke 8:22-25

After Jesus taught these parables to the apostles, he said to them,
"Let's take a break from the noisy crowd, and sail southeast to Gadara."

While they were at sea, a great windstorm arose and the waves threatened to capsize
the boat they were in, but Jesus remained sound asleep on a cushion at the stern.

"Teacher, do you not care if we sink?" they said to Jesus, waking him up.

So Jesus stood and said to the wind and the waves, "Calm down. Be still." And just like that the storm ceased.

Jesus turned to the apostles and said, "Why were you so afraid? I thought you believed in me." And then he went right back to sleep, leaving his friends a little embarrassed and scratching their heads.

They whispered between themselves, "What kind of man is he that even the winds and the sea obey him?"

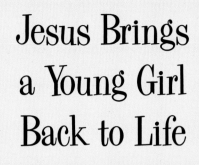

Jesus Brings a Young Girl Back to Life

Matthew 9:18-19,23-26, Mark 5:21-24,35-43, Luke 8:40-42,49-56

When Jesus and his apostles returned to Capernaum from Gadara, there were even more people anxiously waiting for him on the shore.

Just as he got off the boat, an important teacher named Jairus pushed through the crowd and fell at the feet of Jesus.

"My little girl is gravely ill," he said. "Come and lay your hands to heal her."

So the Lord and his friends followed Jairus home, but on the way there Jesus suddenly felt power surging out of him.

It turns out a woman, who was very sick for many years, tried to get hold of him, and when she reached out and grabbed the fringe of Jesus's cloak she was cured of her disease!

"Who touched my clothes?" asked Jesus, looking around to see who did it.

Thinking that she did something wrong, the trembling woman fell to the floor before Jesus and told him the whole truth. Kneeling down to help her up, Jesus said to her with great tenderness, "Daughter, your faith has made you well. You may go home now."

While Jesus was speaking, a man came and said to Jairus, "Your daughter is gone. No need to trouble the Teacher anymore." But Jesus turned around and told him, "Do not fear, only believe."

Arriving at the house, Jesus ordered everybody out but Jairus, the girl's mother, Peter, James, and John. Together they went into the room where the girl was.

"*Talitha, cumi,*" the Lord told the girl while gently holding her hand (which means "Little girl, rise"). So the girl got up and walked, and Jesus asked her parents to give her something to eat.

Jesus Feeds Five Thousand People

Matthew 14:13-21, Mark 6:30-44, Luke 9:10-17, John 6:1-15

Jesus continued to teach and heal the people in Capernaum, while the apostles did the same in other towns of Galilee. They were so busy coming and going from one town to the next, they barely stopped to eat.

So one day, when all of his friends were back to tell him what they did in his name, Jesus told them to sail to the nearby town of Bethsaida for a quiet retreat. But over five thousand people chased the boat by land, and they arrived there first. They seemed so lost that, when Jesus saw them, he was moved to teach them about God's plan, and heal those that needed it anyway.

As the sun went down, Jesus noticed that the people were very hungry and told the apostles, "Give them something to eat."

"We can't afford to," replied Philip.

"There's a boy here with five loaves of barley bread and two fish," added Andrew, "but is that enough to feed so many?"

"Ask everyone to sit down on the grass in groups of fifty," said Jesus.

And taking the loaves and the fish, he looked up to heaven and said a blessing. Then he broke the loaves and fish, passing them out to the apostles, who split everything equally among the people.

Everyone ate, and the leftovers were enough to fill twelve baskets with food. But realizing that the satisfied, happy people now wanted to make him king, Jesus sent his friends back home and quietly slipped away to a mountain to pray alone.

Jesus Walks on Water

Matthew 14:22-33, Mark 6:45-52, John 6:16-21

Three or four miles across the sea, as the apostles sailed back towards Capernaum at night, a strong wind began to blow against them, making it very hard to sail through the raging waves.

Jesus saw they were in trouble from atop the mountain and rushed to help them.

When the apostles saw an approaching figure walking on the water, they mistook Jesus for a ghost and were terrified, but the Lord told them, "Be brave, it is me!"

Peter replied, "If it is you, order me to come to you on the water." Jesus said, "Come then," so Peter got out of the boat, and walked in Jesus's direction.

Halfway toward Jesus, the wind and waves made Peter afraid, and as he lost his faith he began to sink. "Lord, save me," he cried out.

"Why do you doubt?" Jesus asked him, as he stretched his hand to take hold of Peter's hand right on time before he sank. When they got into the boat, the wind stopped raging, and everybody returned home safely.

The Transfiguration

Matthew 17:1-8, Mark 9:2-8, Luke 9:28-36

A week later, Jesus took his very best friends, Peter, James, and John, up to a high mountain to pray.

While Jesus was praying, he transformed into a being of pure light. Moses and Elijah appeared and they spoke to Jesus about God's plan, and what he had to do in Jerusalem.

The three apostles were terrified at this awesome sight. Without giving it much thought, Peter said, "Teacher, it is really nice to be here. Let us make three tents: one for you, one for Moses, and another one for Elijah."

Suddenly, they were all covered by a cloud, and Peter, James, and John fell facedown to the ground trembling when they heard a voice saying, "This is my beloved Son; listen to him."

When the voice finished speaking, Jesus touched them, saying, "Get up, do not fear," and they realized Jesus looked normal again, and no one else was there.

They walked down the mountain with Jesus, who asked them not to tell anybody what they saw and heard.

The Lord's Prayer

Matthew 6:5-15, Luke 11:1-13

After they returned home from the mountain, the apostles said to Jesus, "Lord, teach us how to pray."

Jesus said to them, "Do not pray to be seen by others. Instead go into your room, shut the door, and pray simply and honestly, for your Father knows what you need before you ask.

Pray like this:

"Our Father in heaven, hallowed be your name.

Your kingdom come, your will be done, on earth as in heaven.

Give us today our daily bread.

Forgive us our sins as we forgive those who sin against us.

Lead us not into temptation but deliver us from evil."

The Lost Sheep, the Lost Coin, and the Lost Son

Luke 15:1-32

Jesus continued to meet with people like Matthew, who collected money for the Romans. This made the priests and teachers mad at him, so he told them about being lost and found by God.

"A shepherd guides one hundred sheep across a valley, when he realizes one is missing. So he leaves the ninety-nine sheep behind to go after the one that got lost. And when he finds the sheep, he picks it up, and puts it over his shoulders to bring it home, telling his family, 'Be happy for me. I have found my lost sheep!' God rejoices more over one bad person who is sorry, than ninety-nine who don't need any help."

"A woman loses one of her ten silver coins, so she grabs a lamp and sweeps her whole house until she finds that coin. And when she does, she calls her neighbors saying, 'Be glad for me, I found my lost coin!' God is just as happy when a bad person repents."

Jesus had one more story to tell the judgmental priests and teachers.

"A man has two sons. One day the younger one tells him, 'Dad, give me a large amount of money in exchange for my inheritance.' After getting his money, the young son travels to another country where he wastes it all away having fun. One day, that country is struck by disaster, and the only job he can find is feeding pigs at a farm. By then he is so hungry that he wishes he could eat the scraps he feeds the pigs with, but nobody in that country helps him out."

"He finally comes to his senses, and decides to return home," continued Jesus.

"'I will get up and walk back to my homeland, tell Dad I really am sorry, and ask him to hire me to work his fields,' he tells himself before he sets on the road back home."

"While the young man is still far from the family farm, the father sees him in the distance, and runs to hug and kiss him," says Jesus. "Just as the long-lost son begins his apology, the father calls his employees and asks them to quickly bring the best robe to cover him, put a ring on his hand, and sandals on his feet. And while they're at it, the father decides to throw a big barbecue to celebrate the return of his long-lost son."

"And so should you, when a bad person returns to God," Jesus told the priests and teachers.

The Rich Young Man

Matthew 19:16-30, Mark 10:17-31, Luke 18:18-30

The day Jesus left on his final trip to Jerusalem, a rich, young man approached him with a question.

"Teacher, what should I do to receive eternal life?" he asked.

"Why do you ask?" replied Jesus. "You know the commandments: 'Do not kill, Do not covet, Do not steal, Do not lie, Honor your parents, and Love your neighbor as you love yourself.'"

The young man said, "I have kept all of these since I was a boy. What do I still need to do?"

Jesus loved him for keeping the commandments and said, "Sell all you have and give the money to the poor. Then come and follow me." But when the young man heard this, he became sad and left. He couldn't let go of the things he owned.

Jesus felt even more sad for the young man and told his friends, "It is easier for a camel to go through the eye of a needle, than a rich person to follow God's plan."

And Peter said, "Look, we have left everything behind to follow you."

Jesus Brings Lazarus Back to Life

John 11:1-44, 12:1-6

Passing through Jericho, on the way to Jerusalem, Jesus was staying at the home of a money collector named Zacchaeus when he received news that his dear friend Lazarus was ill.

Jesus loved Lazarus and his sisters, Martha and Mary, very much, but people needed to be healed in Jericho so he stayed there for two more days before leaving for Bethany, where his dear friend lived.

The apostles warned Jesus that the priests and teachers were very angry at him for staying at the home of yet another money collector for the Romans, so they

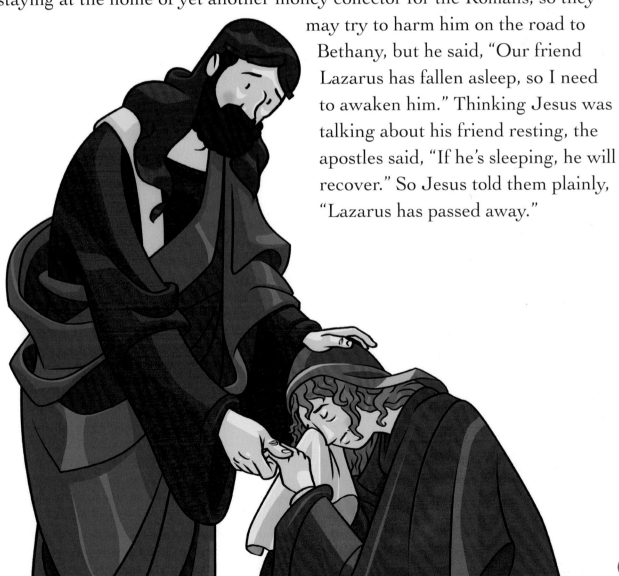

may try to harm him on the road to Bethany, but he said, "Our friend Lazarus has fallen asleep, so I need to awaken him." Thinking Jesus was talking about his friend resting, the apostles said, "If he's sleeping, he will recover." So Jesus told them plainly, "Lazarus has passed away."

When Jesus was on the road to Bethany, Martha came out to meet him and said, "Lord, if you had been here, our brother would not have died." And Jesus replied, "I am the resurrection and the life. Whoever believes in me will never die."

Then Martha went back and told Mary that Jesus was nearby, so Mary came to Jesus and, falling to his feet, she also said, "Lord, if you had been here, our brother would not have died." When he saw Mary weeping, Jesus was deeply moved and cried for his friend as well.

Led to the place where Lazarus was buried, after asking for the tombstone to be removed, Jesus looked up and prayed, "Father, I know you always listen to me, but I say this so the people here will believe that you sent me: Lazarus, come out." And Lazarus came back to life and walked out of the tomb.

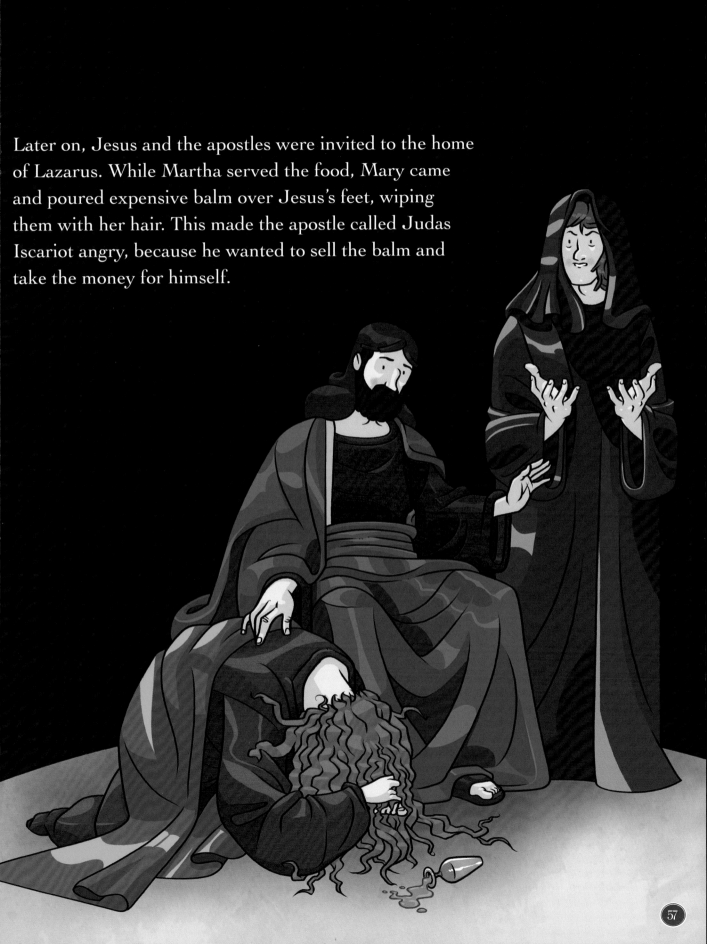

Later on, Jesus and the apostles were invited to the home of Lazarus. While Martha served the food, Mary came and poured expensive balm over Jesus's feet, wiping them with her hair. This made the apostle called Judas Iscariot angry, because he wanted to sell the balm and take the money for himself.

The Talents

Matthew 25:14-30, Luke 19:11-27

Leaving Bethany for Jerusalem, Jesus told his friends the following parable about making the best with the gifts God gave them.

"Before traveling to a faraway land to be crowned king, a nobleman asked his three servants to manage his money while he was away. To the first one, he gave five talents; to the second one, he gave two talents; and to the third one, he gave one talent.

When the newly crowned king returned, he called the three servants to his presence and asked what they did with the riches he entrusted them.

The first servant came forward and said, "Lord, you gave me five talents. I invested those and earned another five."

"Well done! Since you were a good and faithful manager, I will give you authority over ten cities," replied the king.

The second servant then came forward and said, "Lord, you gave me two talents. I put those to work and the profits now fill another two."

"Well done! Since you were a good and faithful manager, I will give you authority over four cities," replied the king.

The third manager came forward and said, "Lord, since you gave me just one talent I was afraid to lose it, so I buried it. Here, I give you back the chest you gave me."

"If you were so afraid you should have put it in the bank, and received the talent back with interest after my return," replied the king.

"Throw this lazy manager out," the king ordered, "and give his talent to the one that made ten."

Jesus Enters Jerusalem

Matthew 21:1-22, Mark 11:1-25, Luke 13:6-9 and 19:28-48, John 12:12-19

Four days before the Passover celebration, Jesus and the apostles arrived at the Mount of Olives ridge to the east of Jerusalem.

They were about to reach a tiny village called Bethphage, when Jesus said to two of his friends, "Go to the village and fetch me a donkey colt you will find tied to a post. If anyone asks why, say, 'The Lord needs it, and will return it right away.'"

It happened just as Jesus told them, so they brought the colt to him, and used their robes as a saddle for Jesus to mount it all the way to Jerusalem.

Fellow travelers began to spread their cloaks and leafy olive branches on the road before the Lord shouting "Hosanna! Blessed is he who comes in the name of the Lord!" when Jesus entered the city.

But Jesus wasn't happy at all. Instead, he wept all the way, because he knew that the people of the city did not believe, and also knew what they were going to do to him there.

When Jesus entered the temple and saw it was filled with people selling animals and not being fair, he got upset and began to drive them all out, saying, "My house should be a house of prayer, but you've made it a place for robbers!"

After all were out, Jesus started to teach about God's plan to everyone who would listen, and this made the priests and teachers furious.

The following morning, Jesus was hungry. He saw a fig tree on the side of the road and went to it. Finding no fruit hanging from its branches he said to it, "May nothing ever grow from you again!" and the tree withered at once.

Another time, Jesus told a parable about a fig tree that didn't bear fruit. The story was a way to explain to his disciples that people who follow God should act in a way that honors God, just like a fig tree should produce figs.

Judas Betrays Jesus

Matthew 26:1-5 and 14-16, Mark 14:1-2 and 10-11, Luke 22:1-6

A couple of days later, while Jesus and his friends were planning the Passover dinner, the priests and teachers gathered at the palace of high-priest Caiaphas.

They were angry at Jesus because of the things he did, like staying at the homes of tax-collectors and kicking merchants out of the temple.

They were upset because of the miracles that Jesus did, like raising Lazarus from the grave—and they didn't like Lazarus very much either!

But they especially feared that Jesus was teaching about God's plan, and that the people's love for Jesus was greater than the respect they held for them, so these men decided to secretly arrest Jesus and kill him after the Passover supper, so those who loved Jesus wouldn't revolt.

Then somebody knocked at the door while they were scheming.

It was the apostle Judas Iscariot, still angry with Jesus for not allowing him to sell Mary's balm (and pocket the money). So the priests and teachers promised Judas a reward of thirty silver coins if he would deliver Jesus to them at the right time.

The Last Supper

Matthew 26:17-29, Mark 14:12-25, Luke 22:7-30, John 13:1-35

On Passover day, Jesus said to his friends, "On the streets of Jerusalem, you will see a man carrying a jar of water. Follow him to his house and tell him I say, 'Where is my guest room, where I may eat the Passover meal with my apostles?' And he will show you a large room upstairs, furnished and ready."

Jesus's friends found the man and the guest room just as Jesus said they would, and they prepared everything.

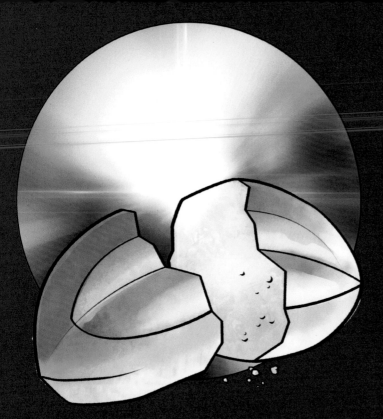

In the evening, Jesus arrived with the twelve and they sat for supper. Jesus took the bread, blessed it, broke it, and shared the pieces with his friends saying, "This is my body."

Then he took a cup and saying thanks he shared it with the apostles saying, "This is my blood, which I pour out for many. Do this to remember me."

After sharing the meal, the apostles began to argue about which one of them was the greatest, so Jesus took off his robe, tied a towel around his waist, and rose to pour water into a basin, which he used to wash the feet of each of his friends.

When Jesus was done, he said to them, "Do you understand what I have done? If I, your Lord and Teacher do this for you, so you should serve one another."

Jesus Prays at Gethsemane

Matthew 26:36-56, Mark 14:26,32-52,
Luke 22:39-53, John 18:1-12

At night, Jesus went with Peter, James, and John to the garden of Gethsemane, an oil mill plot at the foot of the Mount of Olives where Jesus used to pray with his friends.

On the way, Peter assured Jesus he would never leave him. Jesus looked at Peter with sad eyes and said, "Before the rooster crows at the break of dawn, you will deny me three times." And Peter, James, and John all insisted they would do no such thing.

When they arrived at the garden, Jesus said to his friends, "Sit here and keep watch while I pray."

Going farther ahead, Jesus fell on his face and prayed, "Father, if you are willing, please take this cup of suffering away from me, but let your will be done and not mine."

He was in such pain, that an angel appeared to soothe him, but when he got up he found his friends deeply asleep, so he woke them.

"Could you not keep watch for an hour? The one who betrayed me is already here," Jesus said.

That's when Judas Iscariot appeared, followed by armed guards sent by the priests and teachers.

Judas came up to Jesus and said, "Greetings, Teacher!" kissing him. That was the signal the guards waited for to arrest Jesus.

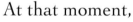

At that moment, Peter attacked one of the guards, but Jesus said, "No more violence!" Then he turned to the arrest party and said, "It is me that you want, let these men go." So they let the apostles go.

Meanwhile, a young follower of Jesus witnessed everything in hiding.

He followed the guards as they bound and dragged Jesus away. When a guard saw and tried to catch him, He ran away and all the guard could grab was his clothes.

Peter Denies Jesus

Matthew 26:57-75, Mark 14:53-72, Luke 22:54-71, John 18:15-27

Jesus was brought to the palace of high priest Caiaphas, where the guards mocked and beat him.

Meanwhile, Peter found his way into the palace. It was cold, and when he went to warm himself by the courtyard fire, a servant girl pointed at him and told the mob, "This man was with Jesus the Galilean." But Peter denied it saying, "Woman, I do not know him."

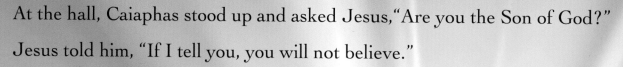

At the hall, Caiaphas stood up and asked Jesus, "Are you the Son of God?"

Jesus told him, "If I tell you, you will not believe."

Caiaphas yelled back at him, "In the name of God, tell us if you're the Christ, his son!"

And Jesus said, "You said it. But I also tell you that you will see me sitting at the right hand of God, and coming from above to judge you."

Caiaphas tore his robes and screamed, "Blasphemy! He deserves death!"

At the same time, another servant girl saw Peter and said to the bystanders, "This man was with Jesus of Nazareth." And again Peter said, "I do not know the man."

Then a bystander grabbed Peter by the sleeve and said, "You have a Galilean accent, so you must be one of his friends!"

And Peter told him, "I tell you I do not know the man, I swear!" and as he finished uttering those words, the rooster crowed. Peter suddenly remembered that Jesus foretold his denial, and he ran away in tears.

Jesus Before Pilate

Matthew 27:2-31, Mark 15:1-20, Luke 23:1-25, John 18:28-39 and 19:16

Early in the morning, the priests and the teachers sent Jesus to Roman Governor Pontius Pilate to be legally tried.

When Jesus stood before him at his headquarters, Pilate asked him, "Are you the King of the Jews?" And Jesus answered, "You say that I am a king. I have come to this world to bear witness to the truth."

"What truth?" asked Pilate. After Jesus remained silent, he went out and told the priests and teachers, "I don't find this man guilty of anything. I will have him punished, and then released."

But the priests and teachers demanded that Pilate release a criminal known as Barabbas instead, as that was Pilate's custom during Passover.

Pilate asked them, "And what should I do to the King of the Jews?" And they shouted, "Crucify him, crucify him, crucify him!"

So Pilate asked for water, and washed his hands before the screaming mob saying, "I am innocent of this man's death."

The Way to the Cross

Matthew 27:27-32, Mark 15:21-32, Luke 23:26-31

Pilate then ordered Jesus to be scourged and executed. After hurting Jesus, the soldiers twisted together a crown of thorns and put it on his head, and then they made him wear a purple robe, before they insulted Jesus saying, "All hail the king!"

After this, they took the purple cloak away and led Jesus out to crucify him, but Jesus was so badly hurt that he could barely walk, let alone carry the heavy crossbeam all the way to Golgotha, or "skull hill," where rebels against Rome were executed.

So the soldiers forced a passerby named Simon, a man from the town of Cyrene, in North Africa, to help Jesus carry the cross.

As Jesus and Simon walked up to Golgotha, some brave women who loved Jesus trailed behind them crying, but Jesus turned around and said to them, "Daughters of Jerusalem, do not cry for me, but for yourselves and your children."

The Crucifixion

Matthew 27:33-60, Mark 15:22-46, Luke 23:32-54, John 19:19-37

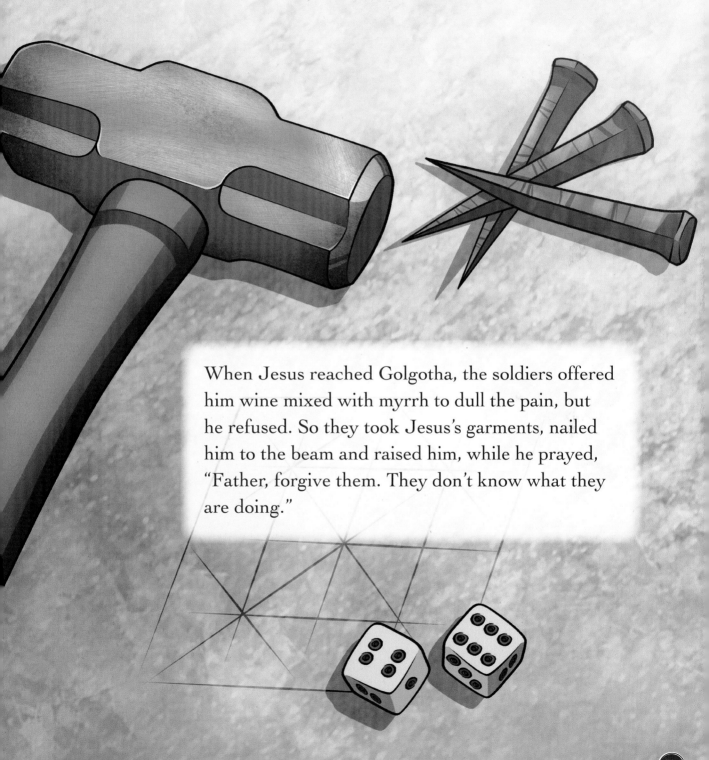

When Jesus reached Golgotha, the soldiers offered him wine mixed with myrrh to dull the pain, but he refused. So they took Jesus's garments, nailed him to the beam and raised him, while he prayed, "Father, forgive them. They don't know what they are doing."

Two bandits also got crucified alongside Jesus. One of them ridiculed Jesus, but the other said to him, "Do you not fear God? We're being punished for our crimes, but this man did nothing wrong." Then he said to Jesus, "Remember me when you go to heaven." And Jesus replied, "Today, you will join me in paradise."

At noon, the sun's light failed and darkness covered the whole land, and after three hours of pain Jesus lamented, "My God, my God, why do you leave me alone?"

Then he said, "I am thirsty," and someone dunked a sponge in sour wine, perched it on a stick, and gave him that awful drink.

At three in the afternoon, Jesus finally cried out, "It is over. Father, my life is in your hands!" and gave up. Right at that moment, an earthquake shook Jerusalem, and the soldiers' commander said, "He really was the Son of God."

Jesus Is Buried

Matthew 27:57-60, Mark 15:42-46,
Luke 23:50-54, John 19:38-42

One of the priests was secretly a friend of Jesus who didn't take part in the illegal arrest and interrogation at the high priest's palace.
His name was Joseph of Arimathea, and he went to Pilate right away to ask for permission to bury the Lord.

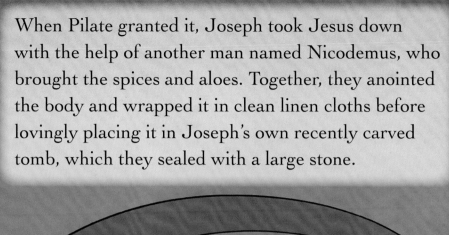

When Pilate granted it, Joseph took Jesus down with the help of another man named Nicodemus, who brought the spices and aloes. Together, they anointed the body and wrapped it in clean linen cloths before lovingly placing it in Joseph's own recently carved tomb, which they sealed with a large stone.

The Resurrection

Matthew 28:1-10, Mark 16:1-8, Luke 24:1-12, John 20: 1-18

Before the sun came up in the early Sunday morning, the women went to the tomb, with more spices and ointments for the body of Jesus.

When they got inside, they saw an angel in bright white clothing sitting on the right, and they were shocked.

Most of the terrified women scrambled out of the tomb and ran to tell the apostles, but Mary, a follower from the village of Magdala, in Galilee, froze outside the tomb in shock.

A man came to her and asked, "Woman, why are you weeping? Who are you looking for?" Taking him for the groundskeeper, she said, "If you have moved his body, tell me where it is so I may take him away."

When the man said, "Mary," she immediately recognized him as Jesus and jumped to hug him, but Jesus said, "Do not cling to me, but go tell my brothers I will see them in Galilee soon."

When the women told Peter and John about the empty tomb, they both ran to it. Since John was younger he arrived first, crawling inside to find the linen cloths lying there. When Peter arrived and stooped in, he also noticed the head linen was folded on the side, so both men believed even if they didn't completely understand how or why.

The Road to Emmaus

Luke 24:13-35

Later that day, two followers of Jesus walked from Jerusalem to the nearby village of Emmaus. They were very sad and talked about what happened to Jesus, when a stranger caught up with them on the road.

He asked them, "What are you talking about?"

"Are you the only pilgrim in town who doesn't know what happened on Friday?" they replied. And they proceeded to tell him about all that Jesus had said and done, and how the priests and teachers delivered him to the Romans to get him killed out of jealousy and fear.

"Now the women are saying they found the tomb empty and talked to an angel," they continued. "When the apostles ran to check on the tomb they, too, found it empty. Not an angel to be found."

So the pilgrim explained to them, "Don't you get it? Moses and the prophets foretold that the Christ would suffer like this before he resurrected and went to heaven." So when they reached the village, the followers of Jesus urged this man to stay with them.

That night, when they were at the table, the stranger took the bread, then blessed, broke, and passed its pieces to them; and at that moment they realized he was none other than Jesus himself, before he vanished from sight!

The Breakfast

John 21:1-14

Some time after the events in Jerusalem, Peter, Thomas, Nathanael, James, John, and two other apostles returned home to Galilee.

One evening, Peter told them, "I'm going fishing." The other apostles went fishing with him, but after spending all night at sea they caught nothing.

Early the next morning, as they approached the shore on the boat they saw a man walking on the beach who asked them, "Do you have any fish?"

They replied "no," so the stranger told them, "Cast the net on the right side of the boat and you will find some," and they caught so many that they couldn't haul the net in. Then John realized who this man really was and told Peter, "It is the Lord!"

The moment Peter heard that, he jumped into the sea and swam ashore, followed by the apostles on the boat. When they reached the land, they saw a charcoal fire already lit, with fish on it, and bread on the side.

"Bring some of the fish you caught, too," said Jesus, "and let's have breakfast." He broke and gave them the bread, and did the same with the fish.

When they finished eating, Jesus said to Peter, "Simon, do you love me more than these?" And Peter said, "Yes Lord, you know that I love you." So Jesus told him, "Feed my lambs."

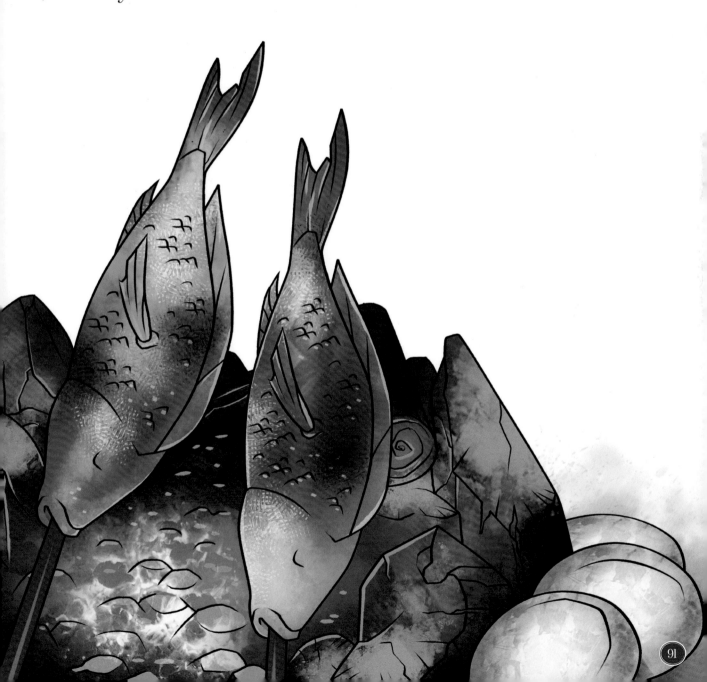

Jesus asked Peter again, "Simon, do you love me?" And Peter again replied, "Yes Lord, you know that I love you." So Jesus told him, "Tend my sheep."

Jesus asked Peter a third time, "Simon, do you love me?" And from the bottom of his heart Peter replied, "Lord, you know everything, you know that I love you."

"When you were young you did as you pleased, but when you get old you will die like I did," Jesus told Peter. "Now follow me."

And that's what Peter did.

The Great Commission

Matthew 28:16-20, Acts 1:6-8

When all the eleven finally gathered in Galilee, they joined Jesus up on a mountain and worshiped him.

Jesus commanded them as follows:

"Go and make disciples of all nations, baptizing them in the name of the Father, and of the Son, and of the Holy Spirit. Teach them to apply all that I have taught you. I am with you always."

"Lord, will you return to us soon?" they asked. But Jesus replied, "It is not for you to know when the Father has decided that my return will happen, but you will receive power from the Holy Spirit to be my witnesses in Jerusalem, and in all Judea and Samaria, and to the ends of the earth."

The Ascension
Acts 1:10-11

While the apostles looked on, Jesus was then lifted up and disappeared behind the clouds.

Since the apostles kept gazing into heaven, two angels in shining white robes appeared and told them, "Men of Galilee, why do you keep looking up?

This Jesus, who was taken into heaven, will come back in the same way as you saw him go."

And so, the apostles returned to Jerusalem to wait for the coming of the Holy Spirit to help them out with their mission . . . but that is another story.

ALSO AVAILABLE FROM
GOOD BOOKS

5-Minute
Bible
Stories

Stories
from the
Old and New
Testament